The Pie That Jack Made
El pastel que hizo Jack

by Liza Charlesworth

The Pie That Jack Made

El pastel que hizo Jack

by Liza Charlesworth

No part of this publication can be reproduced in whole or in part, or stored in a retrieval system, or transmitted in any form or by any means, electronic, mechanical, photocopying, recording, or otherwise, without written permission of the publisher. For permission, write to Scholastic Inc., 557 Broadway, New York, NY 10012.

ISBN: 978-1-338-70333-7
Illustrated by Anne Kennedy
Copyright © 2020 by Liza Charlesworth. All rights reserved.
Published by Scholastic Inc., 557 Broadway, New York, NY 10012

10 9 8 7 6 5 4 3 68 22 23 24 25 26/0

Printed in Jiaxing, China. First printing, June 2020.

This is Jack's seed.

Esta es la semilla de Jack.

He put it in the ground.

La sembró en la tierra.

It grew a sprout.

De la semilla nació una plantita.

It grew a flower.

De la plantita nació una flor.

It grew a pumpkin.

De la flor nació una calabaza.

Jack picked the pumpkin.

Jack recogió la calabaza.

Jack made a pumpkin pie.
Yum!

Jack hizo un pastel de calabaza.
¡Qué rico!

English-Spanish
First Little Readers™

ISBN: 978-1-338-70333-7

SCHOLASTIC

www.scholastic.com

Funny Foods
Comidas raras

by Liza Charlesworth

Funny Foods
Comidas raras

by Liza Charlesworth

No part of this publication can be reproduced in whole or in part, or stored in a retrieval system, or transmitted in any form or by any means, electronic, mechanical, photocopying, recording, or otherwise, without written permission of the publisher. For permission, write to Scholastic Inc., 557 Broadway, New York, NY 10012.

ISBN: 978-1-338-70332-0
Illustrated by Anne Kennedy
Copyright © 2020 by Liza Charlesworth. All rights reserved.
Published by Scholastic Inc., 557 Broadway, New York, NY 10012

10 9 8 7 6 5 4 3   68   22 23 24 25 26/0

Printed in Jiaxing, China. First printing, June 2020.

He likes pickles on his pizza.
Yucky, yucky!

A él le gusta la pizza
con pepinillos.
¡Guácatela!

He likes ketchup on his cookie.
Yucky, yucky!

A él le gusta la galleta
con kétchup.
¡Guácatela!

He likes carrots on his cupcake.
Yucky, yucky!

A él le gusta el pastelito
con zanahorias.
¡Guácatela!

He likes sugar on his sandwich.
Yucky, yucky!

A él le gusta el sándwich
con azúcar.
¡Guácatela!

He likes bananas on his burger.
Yucky, yucky!

A él le gusta la hamburguesa
con plátanos.
¡Guácatela!

He likes honey on his hotdog.
Yucky, yucky!

A él le gusta el perrito caliente con miel.
¡Guácatela!

He likes ice cream in his tummy!
Yummy, yummy!

¡A él le gusta su panza
con helado!
¡Ay, qué rico!

English-Spanish
First Little Readers™

ISBN: 978-1-338-70332-0

Scholastic

www.scholastic.com

Round, the Clown
El payaso Redondo

by Liza Charlesworth

Round, the Clown
El payaso Redondo

by Liza Charlesworth

No part of this publication can be reproduced in whole or in part, or stored in a retrieval system, or transmitted in any form or by any means, electronic, mechanical, photocopying, recording, or otherwise, without written permission of the publisher. For permission, write to Scholastic Inc., 557 Broadway, New York, NY 10012.

ISBN: 978-1-338-70331-3
Illustrated by Anne Kennedy
Copyright © 2020 by Liza Charlesworth. All rights reserved.
Published by Scholastic Inc., 557 Broadway, New York, NY 10012

10 9 8 7 6 5 4 3   68   22 23 24 25 26/0

Printed in Jiaxing, China. First printing, June 2020.

Here is a clown.
His name is Round.

Este es un payaso.
Se llama Redondo.

His nose is round.
That is right!

Su nariz es redonda.
¡Así es!

His ball is round.
That is right!

Su pelota es redonda.
¡Así es!

His balloon is round.
That is right!

Su globo es redondo.
¡Así es!

His hoop is round.
That is right!

Su aro es redondo.
¡Así es!

His lollipop is round.
That is right.

Su piruleta es redonda.
¡Así es!

His lollipop is not round now.
That is right!

Su piruleta ya no es redonda.
¡Así es!

English-Spanish
First Little Readers™

SCHOLASTIC

www.scholastic.com

ISBN: 978-1-338-70331-3

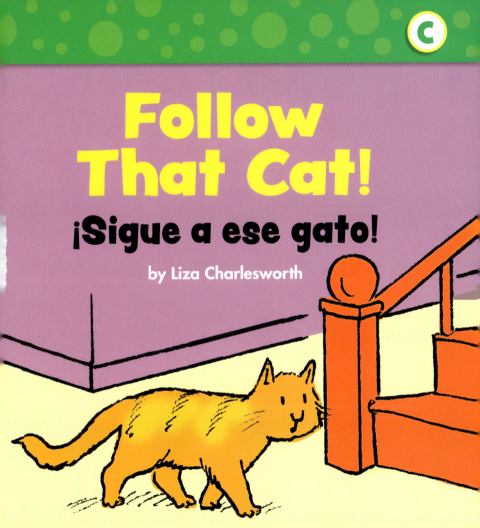

Follow That Cat!
¡Sigue a ese gato!

by Liza Charlesworth

Follow That Cat!
¡Sigue a ese gato!

by Liza Charlesworth

No part of this publication can be reproduced in whole or in part, or stored in a retrieval system, or transmitted in any form or by any means, electronic, mechanical, photocopying, recording, or otherwise, without written permission of the publisher. For permission, write to Scholastic Inc., 557 Broadway, New York, NY 10012.

ISBN: 978-1-338-70330-6
Illustrated by Anne Kennedy
Copyright © 2020 by Liza Charlesworth. All rights reserved.
Published by Scholastic Inc., 557 Broadway, New York, NY 10012

10 9 8 7 6 5 4 3 68 22 23 24 25 26/0

Printed in Jiaxing, China. First printing, June 2020.

Follow that cat!

¡Sigue a ese gato!

Follow that cat to the stairs.
"Meow!"

Sigue a ese gato hasta
las escaleras.
—¡Miau!

Follow that cat to the chairs.
"Meow!"

Sigue a ese gato hasta las sillas.
—¡Miau!

Follow that cat to the toys.
"Meow!"

Sigue a ese gato hasta
los juguetes.
—¡Miau!

Follow that cat to the boys.
"Meow!"

Sigue a ese gato hasta los niños.
—¡Miau!

Follow that cat to the lap.
"Meow!"

Sigue a ese gato hasta el sofá.
—¡Miau!

Watch him curl up to take a nap.
"Purrrrrrrr!"

Mira cómo se acurruca para tomar una siesta.
—¡Purrrrrr!

English-Spanish
First Little Readers™

ISBN: 978-1-338-70330-6

SCHOLASTIC

www.scholastic.com

Counting Bugs
Contar insectos

by Liza Charlesworth

Counting Bugs
Contar insectos

by Liza Charlesworth

No part of this publication can be reproduced in whole or in part, or stored in a retrieval system, or transmitted in any form or by any means, electronic, mechanical, photocopying, recording, or otherwise, without written permission of the publisher. For permission, write to Scholastic Inc., 557 Broadway, New York, NY 10012.

ISBN: 978-1-338-70329-0
Illustrated by Anne Kennedy
Copyright © 2020 by Liza Charlesworth. All rights reserved.
Published by Scholastic Inc., 557 Broadway, New York, NY 10012

10 9 8 7 6 5 4 3 68 22 23 24 25 26/0

Printed in Jiaxing, China. First printing, June 2020.

Let's count bugs in my garden.

Vamos a contar los insectos de mi jardín.

One grasshopper hops.

Un saltamontes salta.

Two butterflies flutter, flutter.

Dos mariposas revolotean, revolotean.

Three worms wiggle, wiggle, wiggle.

Tres gusanitos se contonean,
se contonean, se contonean.

Four ladybugs fly, fly, fly, fly.

Cuatro mariquitas vuelan, vuelan, vuelan, vuelan.

Five spiders creep, creep, creep, creep, creep.

Cinco arañas andan, andan, andan, andan, andan.

But none of them makes a single peep!

Pero ninguno de ellos dice ni pío.

English-Spanish
First Little Readers™

ISBN: 978-1-338-70329-0

SCHOLASTIC

www.scholastic.com

Lunch Crunch
Almuerzo crujiente

by Liza Charlesworth

Lunch Crunch
Almuerzo crujiente

by Liza Charlesworth

No part of this publication can be reproduced in whole or in part, or stored in a retrieval system, or transmitted in any form or by any means, electronic, mechanical, photocopying, recording, or otherwise, without written permission of the publisher. For permission, write to Scholastic Inc., 557 Broadway, New York, NY 10012.

ISBN: 978-1-338-70328-3
Illustrated by Anne Kennedy
Copyright © 2020 by Liza Charlesworth. All rights reserved.
Published by Scholastic Inc., 557 Broadway, New York, NY 10012

10 9 8 7 6 5 4 3   68   22 23 24 25 26/0

Printed in Jiaxing, China. First printing, June 2020.

When I eat lunch,
my crackers go crunch!

Cuando almuerzo,
¡mis galletas saladas crujen!

When I eat lunch,
my carrots go crunch!

Cuando almuerzo,
¡mis zanahorias crujen!

When I eat lunch,
my celery goes crunch!

Cuando almuerzo,
¡mi palito de apio cruje!

When I eat lunch,
my chips go crunch!

Cuando almuerzo,
¡mis papitas crujen!

When I eat lunch,
my apple goes crunch!

Cuando almuerzo,
¡mi manzana cruje!

When I eat lunch,
my cookie goes crunch!

Cuando almuerzo,
¡mi galleta cruje!

When I'm done with lunch,
my bag goes crunch!

Cuando termino mi almuerzo,
¡mi bolsa de papel cruje!

English-Spanish
First Little Readers™

ISBN: 978-1-338-70328-3

SCHOLASTIC

www.scholastic.com

Bubble Shapes
Figuras de burbujas

by Liza Charlesworth

Bubble Shapes
Figuras de burbujas

by Liza Charlesworth

No part of this publication can be reproduced in whole or in part, or stored in a retrieval system, or transmitted in any form or by any means, electronic, mechanical, photocopying, recording, or otherwise, without written permission of the publisher. For permission, write to Scholastic Inc., 557 Broadway, New York, NY 10012.

ISBN: 978-1-338-70327-6
Illustrated by Anne Kennedy
Copyright © 2020 by Liza Charlesworth. All rights reserved.
Published by Scholastic Inc., 557 Broadway, New York, NY 10012

10 9 8 7 6 5 4 3   68   22 23 24 25 26/0

Printed in Jiaxing, China. First printing, June 2020.

SCHOLASTIC

Look at the bubbles I can blow!

¡Mira las burbujas
que puedo hacer!

I can blow a bubble bear
and a bubble chair!

¡Puedo hacer
un oso de burbujas
y una silla de burbujas!

I can blow a bubble dragon
and a bubble wagon!

¡Puedo hacer
un dragón de burbujas
y una carreta de burbujas!

I can blow a bubble star
and a bubble guitar!

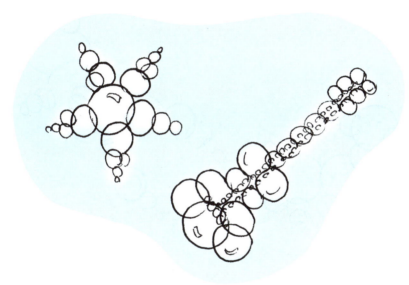

¡Puedo hacer
una estrella de burbujas
y una guitarra de burbujas!

I can blow a bubble dog
and a bubble frog!

¡Puedo hacer
un perro de burbujas
y una rana de burbujas!

I can blow a bubble one
and a bubble sun!

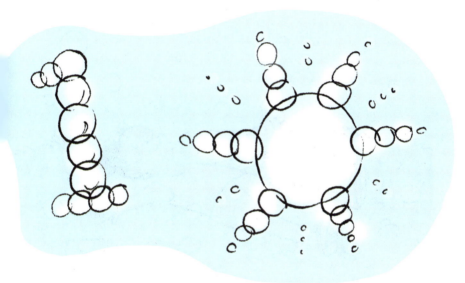

¡Puedo hacer
un uno de burbujas
y un sol de burbujas!

Now my bubble fun is done!

¡Qué divertido es hacer burbujas!

English-Spanish
First Little Readers™

ISBN: 978-1-338-70327-6

Scholastic
www.scholastic.com

All About Dinosaurs
odo sobre los dinosaurios

by Liza Charlesworth

All About Dinosaurs
Todo sobre los dinosaurios

by Liza Charlesworth

No part of this publication can be reproduced in whole or in part, or stored in a retrieval system, or transmitted in any form or by any means, electronic, mechanical, photocopying, recording, or otherwise, without written permission of the publisher. For permission, write to Scholastic Inc., 557 Broadway, New York, NY 10012.

ISBN: 978-1-338-70326-9
Illustrated by Anne Kennedy
Copyright © 2020 by Liza Charlesworth. All rights reserved.
Published by Scholastic Inc., 557 Broadway, New York, NY 10012

10 9 8 7 6 5 4 3   68   22 23 24 25 26/0

Printed in Jiaxing, China. First printing, June 2020.

Some dinosaurs had plates.

Algunos dinosaurios
tenían púas.

Some dinosaurs had horns.

Algunos dinosaurios
tenían cuernos.

Some dinosaurs ate leaves.

Algunos dinosaurios comían hojas.

Some dinosaurs ate meat.

Algunos dinosaurios
comían carne.

Some dinosaurs were as big as a bus.

Algunos dinosaurios eran tan grandes como un autobús.

Some dinosaurs were as small as a chicken.

Algunos dinosaurios eran tan pequeños como un pollo.

How do we know?
Some dinosaurs left bones behind for us to find!

¿Cómo lo sabemos?
Algunos dinosaurios dejaron sus huesos para que nosotros los encontráramos.

English-Spanish
First Little Readers™

ISBN: 978-1-338-70326-9

Scholastic

www.scholastic.com

Make a Pizza
Haz una pizza

by Liza Charlesworth

Make a Pizza
Haz una pizza

by Liza Charlesworth

No part of this publication can be reproduced in whole or in part, or stored in a retrieval system, or transmitted in any form or by any means, electronic, mechanical, photocopying, recording, or otherwise, without written permission of the publisher. For permission, write to Scholastic Inc., 557 Broadway, New York, NY 10012.

ISBN: 978-1-338-70325-2
Illustrated by Anne Kennedy
Copyright © 2020 by Liza Charlesworth. All rights reserved.
Published by Scholastic Inc., 557 Broadway, New York, NY 10012

10 9 8 7 6 5 4 3 68 22 23 24 25 26/0

Printed in Jiaxing, China. First printing, June 2020.

Let's make a pizza.
There are five steps.

Vamos a hacer una pizza.
Hay cinco pasos.

Step one:
Roll out the dough.

Primer paso:
Estirar la masa.

Step two:
Put on the sauce.

Segundo paso:
Poner la salsa.

Step three:
Put on the spice.

Tercer paso:
Echar las especias.

Step four:
Put on the cheese.

Cuarto paso:
Echar el queso.

Step five:
Put it in the oven.

Quinto paso:
Ponerla en el horno.

All done!
May I please have some?

¡Ya está hecha!
¿Me das un pedazo, por favor?

English-Spanish
First Little Readers™

SCHOLASTIC

www.scholastic.com

ISBN: 978-1-338-70325-2

This Little Piggy
Este cerdito

by Liza Charlesworth

This Little Piggy
Este cerdito

by Liza Charlesworth

No part of this publication can be reproduced in whole or in part, or stored in a retrieval system, or transmitted in any form or by any means, electronic, mechanical, photocopying, recording, or otherwise, without written permission of the publisher. For permission, write to Scholastic Inc., 557 Broadway, New York, NY 10012.

ISBN: 978-1-338-70324-5
Illustrated by Anne Kennedy
Copyright © 2020 by Liza Charlesworth. All rights reserved.
Published by Scholastic Inc., 557 Broadway, New York, NY 10012

10 9 8 7 6 5 4 3 68 22 23 24 25 26/0

Printed in Jiaxing, China. First printing, June 2020.

This little piggy went out shopping.

Este cerdito se fue de compras.

This little piggy met a bear.

Este cerdito conoció a un oso.

This little piggy ate some popcorn.

Este cerdito comió palomitas de maíz.

This little piggy curled her hair.

Esta cerdita se rizó el pelo.

And this little piggy went

Y esta cerdita dijo:

wee, wee, wee

—¡Huy, huy, huy!

up in the air.

en el aire.

English-Spanish
First Little Readers™

SCHOLASTIC

www.scholastic.com

ISBN: 978-1-338-70324-5

Tail Tale
Cuento con cola

by Liza Charlesworth

Tail Tale
Cuento con cola

by Liza Charlesworth

No part of this publication can be reproduced in whole or in part, or stored in a retrieval system, or transmitted in any form or by any means, electronic, mechanical, photocopying, recording, or otherwise, without written permission of the publisher. For permission, write to Scholastic Inc., 557 Broadway, New York, NY 10012.

ISBN: 978-1-338-70323-8
Illustrated by Anne Kennedy
Copyright © 2020 by Liza Charlesworth. All rights reserved.
Published by Scholastic Inc., 557 Broadway, New York, NY 10012

10 9 8 7 6 5 4 3   68   22 23 24 25 26/0

Printed in Jiaxing, China. First printing, June 2020.

Monkey pulled zebra's tail.

El mono le haló
la cola a la cebra.

Then zebra pulled alligator's tail.

Después la cebra le haló
la cola al caimán.

Then alligator pulled giraffe's tail.

Después el caimán le haló la cola a la jirafa.

Then giraffe pulled peacock's tail.

Después la jirafa le haló
la cola al pavo real.

Then peacock pulled snake's tail.

Después el pavo real le haló la cola a la serpiente.

Then snake pulled tiger's tail.

Después la serpiente le haló la cola al tigre.

Then tiger pulled monkey's tail.
Do you think that was fair?

Después el tigre le haló
la cola al mono.
¿Piensas que fue justo?

English-Spanish
First Little Readers™

ISBN: 978-1-338-70323-8

SCHOLASTIC

www.scholastic.com

Eight Arms Are Great
Tener ocho brazos es genial

by Liza Charlesworth

Eight Arms Are Great
Tener ocho brazos es genial

by Liza Charlesworth

No part of this publication can be reproduced in whole or in part, or stored in a retrieval system, or transmitted in any form or by any means, electronic, mechanical, photocopying, recording, or otherwise, without written permission of the publisher. For permission, write to Scholastic Inc., 557 Broadway, New York, NY 10012.

ISBN: 978-1-338-70342-9
Illustrated by Anne Kennedy
Copyright © 2020 by Liza Charlesworth. All rights reserved.
Published by Scholastic Inc., 557 Broadway, New York, NY 10012

10 9 8 7 6 5 4 3   68   22 23 24 25 26/0

Printed in Jiaxing, China. First printing, June 2020.

Eight arms are great!

¡Tener ocho brazos es genial!

Eight arms are great
for reading books!

¡Tener ocho brazos es genial
para leer libros!

Eight arms are great for juggling balls!

¡Tener ocho brazos es genial para hacer malabares!

Eight arms are great
for eating fruit!

¡Tener ocho brazos es genial
para comer fruta!

Eight arms are great
for drawing pictures!

¡Tener ocho brazos es genial
para dibujar!

Eight arms are great for wearing watches!

¡Tener ocho brazos es genial para usar relojes!

Eight arms are great
for waving good-bye!

¡Tener ocho brazos es genial
para despedirse!

English-Spanish
First Little Readers™

ISBN: 978-1-338-70342-9

SCHOLASTIC

www.scholastic.com

Bat Facts
Libro de murciélagos

by Liza Charlesworth

Bat Facts
Libro de murciélagos

by Liza Charlesworth

No part of this publication can be reproduced in whole or in part, or stored in a retrieval system, or transmitted in any form or by any means, electronic, mechanical, photocopying, recording, or otherwise, without written permission of the publisher. For permission, write to Scholastic Inc., 557 Broadway, New York, NY 10012.

ISBN: 978-1-338-70341-2
Illustrated by Anne Kennedy
Copyright © 2020 by Liza Charlesworth. All rights reserved.
Published by Scholastic Inc., 557 Broadway, New York, NY 10012

10 9 8 7 6 5 4 3 68 22 23 24 25 26/0

Printed in Jiaxing, China. First printing, June 2020.

Bats have wings and fur.
That is a fact!

Los murciélagos
tienen alas y pelo.
¡Es un hecho!

Bats live in caves.
That is a fact!

Los murciélagos
viven en cuevas.
¡Es un hecho!

Bats sleep upside down.
That is a fact!

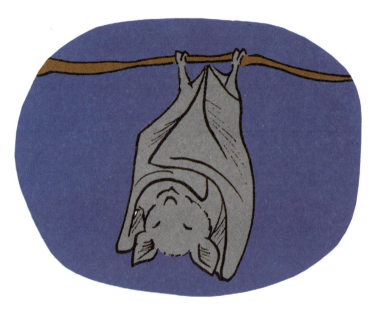

Los murciélagos
duermen cabeza abajo.
¡Es un hecho!

Bats look for food at night.
That is a fact!

Los murciélagos
buscan su comida por la noche.
¡Es un hecho!

Bats eat bugs.
That is a fact!

Los murciélagos
comen insectos.
¡Es un hecho!

Bats clean themselves like cats.
That is a fact!

Los murciélagos
se bañan como los gatos.
¡Es un hecho!

Bats are mammals just like kids.
That is a fact!

Los murciélagos
son mamíferos como los niños.
¡Es un hecho!

English-Spanish
First Little Readers™

ISBN: 978-1-338-70341-2

Scholastic
www.scholastic.com

Snow Tracks
Huellas en la nieve

by Liza Charlesworth

Snow Tracks
Huellas en la nieve

by Liza Charlesworth

No part of this publication can be reproduced in whole or in part, or stored in a retrieval system, or transmitted in any form or by any means, electronic, mechanical, photocopying, recording, or otherwise, without written permission of the publisher. For permission, write to Scholastic Inc., 557 Broadway, New York, NY 10012.

ISBN: 978-1-338-70340-5
Illustrated by Anne Kennedy
Copyright © 2020 by Liza Charlesworth. All rights reserved.
Published by Scholastic Inc., 557 Broadway, New York, NY 10012

10 9 8 7 6 5 4 3   68   22 23 24 25 26/0

Printed in Jiaxing, China. First printing, June 2020.

Who left these tracks in the snow?
It was a horse on the go!

¿Quién dejó estas huellas
en la nieve?
¡Fue un caballo en marcha!

Who left these tracks in the snow?
It was a deer on the go!

¿Quién dejó estas huellas
en la nieve?
¡Fue un ciervo en marcha!

Who left these tracks in the snow?
It was a duck on the go!

¿Quién dejó estas huellas
en la nieve?
¡Fue un pato en marcha!

Who left these tracks in the snow?
It was a fox on the go!

¿Quién dejó estas huellas
en la nieve?
¡Fue un zorro en marcha!

Who left these tracks in the snow?
It was a dog on the go!

¿Quién dejó estas huellas
en la nieve?
¡Fue un perro en marcha!

Who left these tracks in the snow?
It was a rabbit on the go!

¿Quién dejó estas huellas
en la nieve?
¡Fue un conejo en marcha!

Who left these tracks in the snow?
It was a kid on the go!

¿Quién dejó estas huellas
en la nieve?
¡Fue un niño en marcha!

English-Spanish
First Little Readers™

ISBN: 978-1-338-70340-5

Scholastic

www.scholastic.com

Lots of Legs
Muchas patas

by Liza Charlesworth

Lots of Legs
Muchas patas

by Liza Charlesworth

No part of this publication can be reproduced in whole or in part, or stored in a retrieval system, or transmitted in any form or by any means, electronic, mechanical, photocopying, recording, or otherwise, without written permission of the publisher. For permission, write to Scholastic Inc., 557 Broadway, New York, NY 10012.

ISBN: 978-1-338-70339-9
Illustrated by Anne Kennedy
Copyright © 2020 by Liza Charlesworth. All rights reserved.
Published by Scholastic Inc., 557 Broadway, New York, NY 10012

10 9 8 7 6 5 4 3 68 22 23 24 25 26/0

Printed in Jiaxing, China. First printing, June 2020.

How many legs does
a snake have?
A snake has no legs.

¿Cuántas patas tiene
la serpiente?
La serpiente no tiene patas.

How many legs does a girl have?
A girl has 2 legs.

¿Cuántas piernas tiene la niña?
La niña tiene 2 piernas.

How many legs does
a horse have?
A horse has 4 legs.

¿Cuántas patas tiene el caballo?
El caballo tiene 4 patas.

How many legs does an ant have?
An ant has 6 legs.

¿Cuántas patas tiene la hormiga?
La hormiga tiene 6 patas.

How many legs does
a spider have?
A spider has 8 legs.

¿Cuántas patas tiene la araña?
La araña tiene 8 patas.

How many legs does
a centipede have?
A centipede has 30 legs.

¿Cuántas patas tiene el ciempiés?
El ciempiés tiene 30 patas.

My, oh, my!
That is a lot of shoes to tie!

¡Ay, pobrecito,
cuántos zapatos tiene que amarrarse!

English-Spanish
First Little Readers™

SCHOLASTIC
www.scholastic.com

ISBN: 978-1-338-70339

Polka Dot World
Un mundo de lunares

by Liza Charlesworth

Polka Dot World
Un mundo de lunares

by Liza Charlesworth

No part of this publication can be reproduced in whole or in part, or stored in a retrieval system, or transmitted in any form or by any means, electronic, mechanical, photocopying, recording, or otherwise, without written permission of the publisher. For permission, write to Scholastic Inc., 557 Broadway, New York, NY 10012.

ISBN: 978-1-338-70338-2
Illustrated by Anne Kennedy
Copyright © 2020 by Liza Charlesworth. All rights reserved.
Published by Scholastic Inc., 557 Broadway, New York, NY 10012

10 9 8 7 6 5 4 3   68   22 23 24 25 26/0

Printed in Jiaxing, China. First printing, June 2020.

SCHOLASTIC

There are polka dots
on this mouse!

¡Este ratón tiene lunares!

There are polka dots on this house!

¡Esta casa tiene lunares!

There are polka dots
on this fish!

¡Este pez tiene lunares!

There are polka dots
on this dish!

¡Este plato tiene lunares!

There are polka dots
on this dog!

¡Este perro tiene lunares!

There are polka dots
on this log!

¡Este tronco tiene lunares!

There are polka dots
on this bee!
There are even polka dots
on me!

¡Esta abeja tiene lunares!
¡Hasta yo tengo lunares!

English-Spanish
First Little Readers™

ISBN: 978-1-338-70338-

SCHOLASTIC

www.scholastic.com

9 781338 703382

The Teeny Tiny Man
Un hombre muy pequeñito

by Liza Charlesworth

The Teeny Tiny Man
Un hombre muy pequeñito

by Liza Charlesworth

No part of this publication can be reproduced in whole or in part, or stored in a retrieval system, or transmitted in any form or by any means, electronic, mechanical, photocopying, recording, or otherwise, without written permission of the publisher. For permission, write to Scholastic Inc., 557 Broadway, New York, NY 10012.

ISBN: 978-1-338-70337-5
Illustrated by Anne Kennedy
Copyright © 2020 by Liza Charlesworth. All rights reserved.
Published by Scholastic Inc., 557 Broadway, New York, NY 10012

10 9 8 7 6 5 4 3 68 22 23 24 25 26/0

Printed in Jiaxing, China. First printing, June 2020.

SCHOLASTIC

This is a teeny tiny man.

Este es un hombre muy pequeñito.

This is his teeny tiny wife.

Esta es su esposa muy pequeñita.

This is his teeny tiny son.

Este es su hijo muy pequeñito.

This is his teeny tiny daughter.

Esta es su hija muy pequeñita.

This is his teeny tiny cat.

Este es su gato muy pequeñito.

They all live together in this teeny tiny house…

Todos viven juntos en esta casa muy pequeñita…

right next door
to a GIANT mouse!

¡al lado de un ratón GIGANTE!

English-Spanish
First Little Readers™

SCHOLASTIC

www.scholastic.com

ISBN: 978-1-338-70337-

Giant Friends
Amigos gigantes

by Liza Charlesworth

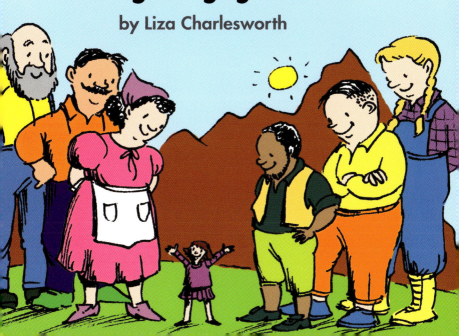

Giant Friends
Amigos gigantes

by Liza Charlesworth

No part of this publication can be reproduced in whole or in part, or stored in a retrieval system, or transmitted in any form or by any means, electronic, mechanical, photocopying, recording, or otherwise, without written permission of the publisher. For permission, write to Scholastic Inc., 557 Broadway, New York, NY 10012.

ISBN: 978-1-338-70336-8
Illustrated by Anne Kennedy
Copyright © 2020 by Liza Charlesworth. All rights reserved.
Published by Scholastic Inc., 557 Broadway, New York, NY 10012

10 9 8 7 6 5 4 3 68 22 23 24 25 26/0

Printed in Jiaxing, China. First printing, June 2020.

SCHOLASTIC

I met a giant who was
as tall as a giraffe.

Conocí a un gigante que era
tan alto como una jirafa.

I met a giant who was
as tall as a tree.

Conocí a una gigante que era
tan alta como un árbol.

I met a giant who was
as tall as a house.

Conocí a un gigante que era
tan alto como una casa.

I met a giant who was
as tall as a building.

Conocí a una gigante que era
tan alta como un edificio.

I met a giant who was as tall as a mountain.

Conocí a un gigante que era tan alto como una montaña.

And as you can see…

Y como puedes ver…

It was hard for him
to shake hands with me!

¡Le era muy difícil darme
la mano!

English-Spanish
First Little Readers™

ISBN: 978-1-338-70336-8

Scholastic
www.scholastic.com

Hot Dog, Hot Dog
Perrito caliente

by Liza Charlesworth

Hot Dog, Hot Dog
Perrito caliente

by Liza Charlesworth

No part of this publication can be reproduced in whole or in part, or stored in a retrieval system, or transmitted in any form or by any means, electronic, mechanical, photocopying, recording, or otherwise, without written permission of the publisher. For permission, write to Scholastic Inc., 557 Broadway, New York, NY 10012.

ISBN: 978-1-338-70335-1
Illustrated by Anne Kennedy
Copyright © 2020 by Liza Charlesworth. All rights reserved.
Published by Scholastic Inc., 557 Broadway, New York, NY 10012

10 9 8 7 6 5 4 3 68 22 23 24 25 26/0

Printed in Jiaxing, China. First printing, June 2020.

SCHOLASTIC

Hot dog, hot dog on my plate,
boy, oh, boy, you sure look great!

Perrito caliente en mi plato,
¡uy, qué rico te ves!

Hamburger, hamburger
on my plate,
boy, oh, boy, you sure look great!

Hamburguesa en mi plato,
¡uy, qué rica te ves!

French fries, french fries
on my plate,
boy, oh, boy, you sure look great!

Papas fritas en mi plato,
¡uy, qué ricas se ven!

Salad, salad on my plate,
boy, oh, boy, you sure look great!

Ensalada en mi plato,
¡uy, qué rica te ves!

Watermelon, watermelon on my plate,
boy, oh, boy, you sure look great

Sandía en mi plato,
¡uy, qué rica te ves!

Cookie, cookie on my plate,
boy, oh, boy, you sure look great!

Galleta en mi plato,
¡uy, qué rica te ves!

Nothing, nothing on my plate,
boy, oh, boy, my tummy aches!

No queda nada en mi plato,
¡uy, que dolor de panza!

English-Spanish
First Little Readers™

ISBN: 978-1-338-70335-

SCHOLASTIC

www.scholastic.com

Squares Are Everywhere
uadrados por todas partes

by Liza Charlesworth

Squares Are Everywhere
Cuadrados por todas partes

by Liza Charlesworth

No part of this publication can be reproduced in whole or in part, or stored in a retrieval system, or transmitted in any form or by any means, electronic, mechanical, photocopying, recording, or otherwise, without written permission of the publisher. For permission, write to Scholastic Inc., 557 Broadway, New York, NY 10012.

ISBN: 978-1-338-70334-4
Illustrated by Anne Kennedy
Copyright © 2020 by Liza Charlesworth. All rights reserved.
Published by Scholastic Inc., 557 Broadway, New York, NY 10012

10 9 8 7 6 5 4 3 68 22 23 24 25 26/0

Printed in Jiaxing, China. First printing, June 2020.

There is one square on this bear.
Can you find it?

Hay un cuadrado en este oso.
¿Lo ves?

There are two squares
on this chair.
Can you find them?

Hay dos cuadrados en este sillón.
¿Los ves?

There are three squares
on this jar.
Can you find them?

Hay tres cuadrados en este pote.
¿Los ves?

There are four squares on this car.
Can you find them?

Hay cuatro cuadrados
en este carro.
¿Los ves?

There are five squares
on this shelf.
Can you find them?

Hay cinco cuadrados
en este estante.
¿Los ves?

There are six squares on this elf.
Can you find them?

Hay seis cuadrados
en este duende.
¿Los ves?

Squares are everywhere!
Can you find them?

¡Hay cuadrados por todas partes!
¿Los ves?

English-Spanish
First Little Readers™

ISBN: 978-1-338-70334-

9 781338 703344

SCHOLASTIC

www.scholastic.com

Surprises
Sorpresas

by Liza Charlesworth

Surprises
Sorpresas

by Liza Charlesworth

No part of this publication can be reproduced in whole or in part, or stored in a retrieval system, or transmitted in any form or by any means, electronic, mechanical, photocopying, recording, or otherwise, without written permission of the publisher. For permission, write to Scholastic Inc., 557 Broadway, New York, NY 10012.

ISBN: 978-1-338-70343-6
Illustrated by Anne Kennedy
Copyright © 2020 by Liza Charlesworth. All rights reserved.
Published by Scholastic Inc., 557 Broadway, New York, NY 10012

10 9 8 7 6 5 4 3 68 22 23 24 25 26/0

Printed in Jiaxing, China. First printing, June 2020.

Can you guess what is in this big box?

¿Adivinas qué hay en la caja grande?

Surprise!
It is a computer.

¡Sorpresa!
Es una computadora.

Can you guess what is in this very big box?

¿Adivinas qué hay
en la caja muy grande?

Surprise!
It is a bike.

¡Sorpresa!
Es una bicicleta.

Can you guess what is in this very, very big box?

¿Adivinas qué hay
en la caja muy,
pero que muy grande?

Surprise!
It is an elephant!

¡Sorpresa!
¡Es un elefante!

Wow!
That is just what I wanted!

¡Ajá!
¡Eso era lo que yo quería!

English-Spanish
First Little Readers™

ISBN: 978-1-338-70343-

Scholastic

www.scholastic.com

9 781338 703436

Clay Play
Juego con plastilina

by Liza Charlesworth

Clay Play
Juego con plastilina

by Liza Charlesworth

No part of this publication can be reproduced in whole or in part, or stored in a retrieval system, or transmitted in any form or by any means, electronic, mechanical, photocopying, recording, or otherwise, without written permission of the publisher. For permission, write to Scholastic Inc., 557 Broadway, New York, NY 10012.

ISBN: 978-1-338-70344-3
Illustrated by Anne Kennedy
Copyright © 2020 by Liza Charlesworth. All rights reserved.
Published by Scholastic Inc., 557 Broadway, New York, NY 10012

10 9 8 7 6 5 4 3 68 22 23 24 25 26/0

Printed in Jiaxing, China. First printing, June 2020.

See what I made out of clay.

Mira lo que hice con plastilina.

I made a bird.
It can soar!

Hice un pájaro.
¡Puede volar!

I made a lion.
It can roar!

Hice un león.
¡Puede rugir!

I made a robot.
It can walk!

Hice un robot.
¡Puede caminar!

I made a puppet.
It can talk!

Hice una marioneta.
¡Puede hablar!

I made a snake.
It can stretch!

Hice una serpiente.
¡Se puede alargar!

Oops!
I also made a mess.

¡Ay!
También hice un desorden.

English-Spanish
First Little Readers™

SCHOLASTIC

www.scholastic.com

ISBN: 978-1-338-70344-

Draw a Pig
Dibuja un cerdo

by Liza Charlesworth

Draw a Pig
Dibuja un cerdo

by Liza Charlesworth

No part of this publication can be reproduced in whole or in part, or stored in a retrieval system, or transmitted in any form or by any means, electronic, mechanical, photocopying, recording, or otherwise, without written permission of the publisher. For permission, write to Scholastic Inc., 557 Broadway, New York, NY 10012.

ISBN: 978-1-338-70345-0
Illustrated by Anne Kennedy
Copyright © 2020 by Liza Charlesworth. All rights reserved.
Published by Scholastic Inc., 557 Broadway, New York, NY 10012

10 9 8 7 6 5 4 3   68   22 23 24 25 26/0

Printed in Jiaxing, China. First printing, June 2020.

Want to draw a pig with me?

¿Quieres dibujar un cerdo conmigo?

Draw three circles.
It's easy!

Dibuja tres círculos.
¡Es fácil!

Draw four dots.
It's as easy as can be!

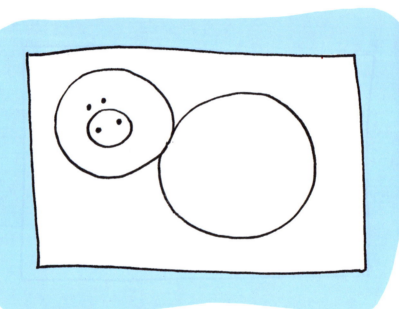

Dibuja cuatro puntitos.
Más fácil, ¡imposible!

Draw two triangles.
It's as easy as can be!

Dibuja dos triángulos.
Más fácil, ¡imposible!

Draw two squares.
It's as easy as can be!

Dibuja dos cuadrados.
Más fácil, ¡imposible!

Draw one curly line.
It's as easy as can be!

Dibuja un rizo.
Más fácil, ¡imposible!

Our pig looks great!
Don't you agree?

Nuestro cerdo es muy bonito.
¿No te parece?

English-Spanish
First Little Readers™

ISBN: 978-1-338-70345-

SCHOLASTIC

www.scholastic.com

Monkey Business
Monos felices

by Liza Charlesworth

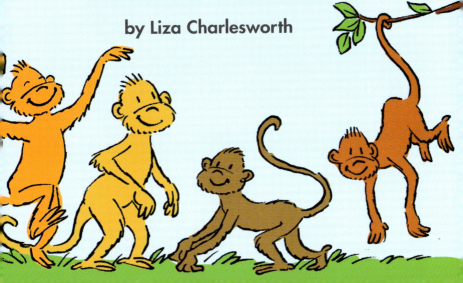

Monkey Business
Monos felices

by Liza Charlesworth

No part of this publication can be reproduced in whole or in part, or stored in a retrieval system, or transmitted in any form or by any means, electronic, mechanical, photocopying, recording, or otherwise, without written permission of the publisher. For permission, write to Scholastic Inc., 557 Broadway, New York, NY 10012.

ISBN: 978-1-338-70346-7
Illustrated by Anne Kennedy
Copyright © 2020 by Liza Charlesworth. All rights reserved.
Published by Scholastic Inc., 557 Broadway, New York, NY 10012

10 9 8 7 6 5 4 3   68   22 23 24 25 26/0

Printed in Jiaxing, China. First printing, June 2020.

Want to learn what monkeys like?

¿Quieres saber lo que les gusta a los monos?

Monkeys like to live in groups.

A los monos les gusta vivir en grupo.

Monkeys like to swing in trees.

A los monos les gusta mecerse en los árboles.

Monkeys like to sleep in trees.

A los monos les gusta dormir en los árboles.

Monkeys like to eat bananas.

A los monos les gusta comer plátanos.

Monkeys like to say "Eee-eee!"

A los monos les gusta decir:
—¡Yi yi!

But monkeys do not like itchy fleas!

¡A los monos no les gustan las pulgas!

English-Spanish
First Little Readers™

ISBN: 978-1-338-70346-

SCHOLASTIC

www.scholastic.com

Shadow Guessing Game
Juego de sombras

by Liza Charlesworth

Shadow Guessing Game
Juego de sombras

by Liza Charlesworth

No part of this publication can be reproduced in whole or in part, or stored in a retrieval system, or transmitted in any form or by any means, electronic, mechanical, photocopying, recording, or otherwise, without written permission of the publisher. For permission, write to Scholastic Inc., 557 Broadway, New York, NY 10012.

ISBN: 978-1-338-70347-4
Illustrated by Anne Kennedy
Copyright © 2020 by Liza Charlesworth. All rights reserved.
Published by Scholastic Inc., 557 Broadway, New York, NY 10012

10 9 8 7 6 5 4 3   68   22 23 24 25 26/0

Printed in Jiaxing, China. First printing, June 2020.

Guess what made this shadow?

¿Adivina de quién es esta sombra?

Did you guess a dog?
You are right!

¿Pensaste que era un perro?
¡Tienes razón!

Guess what made this shadow

Adivina de quién es esta sombra

Did you guess a snake?
You are right!

¿Pensaste que era una serpiente?
¡Tienes razón!

Guess what made this shadow

Adivina de quién es esta sombra

Did you guess a rabbit?
You are wrong.
It was only my fingers!

¿Pensaste que era un conejo?
Te equivocaste.
¡Eran solo mis dedos!

Here is how you do it.
Want to try?

Así es como se hace.
¿Quieres intentarlo?

English-Spanish
First Little Readers™

ISBN: 978-1-338-70347

9 781338 703474